ISBN 978-0-666-99252-9
PIBN 11337066

1 MONTH OF
FREE
READING

at

www.ForgottenBooks.com

By purchasing this book you are eligible for one month membership to ForgottenBooks.com, giving you unlimited access to our entire collection of over 1,000,000 titles via our web site and mobile apps.

To claim your free month visit:
www.forgottenbooks.com/free1337066

Dahlias from Lufkin's

Dahlia List 1929

ANDREW LUFKIN

6 Harrison Avenue
GLOUCESTER, MASS.

Visitors welcome to our trial garden
at above address

TELEPHONE 1027

Greetings - 1929

WITH great pleasure I again present you with my Catalog, this one for 1929.

Won many prizes again this season but the most coveted one was at the Boston Show of the Dahlia Society of New England for the largest and best exhibit—a Wall display of Dahlias, all varieties exhibited, Baskets and Vases of Dahlias all of one kind in a basket. This class had more competition than any other class, all leading growers competing. We wish to thank our many customers for past patronage and trust you will continue favoring us with your orders.

Terms: Cash with order or in advance of shipment.

Guarantee: We guarantee the safe arrival in growing conditions of all orders shipped and will cheerfully replace any that do not so arrive. We will not be held responsible for more than the purchase price. Plants or Tubers not received in good condition must be returned by following mail.

A word about Green Plants

WE offer many varieties in Green Plants at very reasonable prices.

They are good healthy plants hardened off in cold frames, well rooted and ready to go ahead and plant. Furthermore our method of packing plants is such that they will reach you in good growing condition. We prefer Green Plants for several reasons. They produce better flowers as well as better tubers, which are cleaner and free from disease.

Many of our customers who were formerly prejudiced against plants, now order them almost entirely after trying them.

Abbreviations: **C.** signifies Cactus; **Dec.,** Decorative; **H.C.,** Hybrid Cactus; **P.,** Paeony; **S.,** Show

Price List and Description

Adda Patterson (Kemp) H. C.
Tuber Plant

Flowers are pure white and average 8 to 9 ins. in diameter. The plant is a beautiful grower, reaching a height of 7 ft. The large blooms are held well above the foliage, stiff stems that can be cut four or five feet in length, fine for all purposes $3.50

Andreas Hofer (Holland) C.

This Holland origination was one of the most beautiful dahlias seen this season. Rich salmon color with center of gold   3.00

Alice Whittier (Success) H. C.

Heavy primrose, sulphur yellow, deep spike-like petals from 5 to 6 ins. deep and 9 to 10 in diameter   2.50

Amarillo Grande (Broomall) H. D.

Light yellow, compared with Sunny South the petals are broader and the flowers are much larger, in fact they are enormous   2.50

Aztec Glory H. D.

Picric yellow (lemon yellow) large flowers of most unusual formation, held erect on strong stems, as an exhibition yellow decorative, I have never seen its equal, not recommended for cutting. Height 2½ ft. 10.00 $5.00

Anna Marie Frey (Harding) Dec.

A very bright red with all the good qualities of dahlia, Judge Marean. A very fine variety   3.50

Betty Ivins (Fisher & Masson) Dec.

A remarkable flower of huge proportions. Color a rich salmon, overlaid with an amber glow, showing a rosy pink reverse. For a flower of such size it has a remarkable stem   -   7.50   3.50

Baby Pink Beauty (Murphy) Dec.

Color a most beautiful shade of solid pink. Plant, a mass of blooms, held high above the foliage on long wiry stems   7.50   3.50

Becketts Oriental (Murphy) Dec.

The flower on opening is a dark red with golden tips and when matured it is half red and half yellow, good stem and good bloomer   5.00

Berengaria (Holland) Dec.   Tuber Plant

Orange at center, gold tips, very large
flower with good stems   5.00   2.50

Color Sergeant (Hall) Dec.

Saffron colored dahlia of large size and
fine habits, was one of the sensations of
1926. Fine stem   Plants   3.00

City of Trenton (Prentice) Dec.

An autumn colored dahlia, the face of
the petals a rich glowing tangerine,
reverse, crushed strawberry, good stem   7.50   3.50

Charlotte La Frenz (Seal) Dec.

A new decorative of immense size, the
one that all visitors picked. A blending
of gold shades, the perfectly formed
center being a bright gold, shading to a
rich apricot in the outer petals. The
center is very full and the blossom is held
high above a strong sturdy plant   7.50   3.50

Col. Charles A. Lindbergh (Fisher & Masson) H. C.

An early bloomer, very large, a beautiful
rose "Dubarry" overlaid and suffused
with old ivory, shading off to pale gold at
center. Reverse of petals light carmine
pink. A very free bloomer, dark green
foliage, shadings of this flower remind us
of Wizard of Oz   7.50   3.50

Coringa (Broomall-Success) H.D.

Capucine yellow, shaded cornelian red.
The rich coppery orange color of this
dahlia is very attractive, medium large
flowers are held erect on strong but short
stems. As a bedding dahlia it is in a class
by itself   7.50   3.50

Derrill W. Hart (Broomall-Success) Dec.

A real autumn color, copper shading to
henna and brown, some petals also
showing a golden tint. You would have
to see this growing to appreciate it   10.00   5.00

Edna Ferber (Fisher & Masson) H. C.

One of the dahlias that has made a hit in
all parts of the country. Color of this
fine variety is very pleasing, salmon
shading to gold, very large   5.00   2.50

Eagle Rock Beauty (Broomall) H. D.

A beautiful combination of pink and
cream. It is in a class by itself. Every
grower who sees this magnificent flower
will want it. Vigorous growth with good
habit, and strong stems   5.00   2.50

Elinor Vanderveer (Seal) Dec.   Tuber Plant

Large blossoms of glowing satiny pink.
Flowers are of great depth and substance
and are held far above a tall sturdy bush
on exceptionally long stiff stems, one of
the first to bloom   1.50

Elite Glory (Kennedy) Dec.

These were certainly wonderful with us,
every admirer of the large and beautiful
dahlia should have this, most sensational
dahlia of the year.   Monstrous flower of
brilliant rich red shadings.   Blooms and
foliage are gigantic in size   3.50

Eva Cole (Murphy) Dec.

This is one of the finest.   The color is a
striking red and gold, wonderful for
exhibition, can be grown 11 to 12 inches   5.00   2.50

Fort Washington Dec.

A large decorative of dark red, maroon
shade, long stiff stems held far above the
foliage one of the largest, very robust
grower, plant will grow as high as 8 ft.   5.00   2.50

Fandango (Dixon) H. C.

Color, spectrum-red tipped maize-yellow,
back of petals flesh-pink and maize-
yellow.   Stem 8-11 ins., upright.   Size of
flower, 7-8 ins., depth, 3-3½ ins., height 5
ft., large leaf, score 87   5.00   2.50

Firelight (Marean) Dec.

Beautiful large flower carried on stiff
stems, base yellow, points of petals
tipped red, very fine   1.50

Fort Monmouth (Kemp) H. C.

One of the giants of the dahlia world.
Color a rich crimson maroon; I should call
it a rich claret.   The flowers have long
narrow petals well formed, full centered,
of true hybrid cactus type, of enormous
size attaining a diameter of full 13 inches
and are borne on long stiff stems high
above the foliage, and look you right in
the face.   A visitor in the Garden sees
this one before all others   10.00   5.00

Golden Acres (Peck) H. C.

This dahlia is a high grade cut flower of a
most beautiful glistening golden yellow.
Fine stems and very long, not one of the
largest but one of the best   6.00   3.00

Grenadier (Bessie Boston) Dec.

Purplish Maroon shade combined with
silver.   The petals on one side are purple
and on the other, pale silver.   They quill
and turn back.   The whole construction
is unique.   Large flowers and good stems   2.00

	Tuber	Plant

Glory of Monmouth (Kemp) Dec.

New. Eosine pink, shading to strawberry pink at center of petals. Base of petals light orange, a new color combination in dahlias. The plants are semi-dwarf in habit, wide spreading and very sturdy. The flowers are on long strong stems, 6 to 8 ins. in diameter and over 4 ins. in depth. Fine for all purposes   5.00   2.50

General MacRae (Meachen & Sherman) Dec.

One of the best. The face of the petals is apricot buff suffused with gold and the reverse, light coral red, a beautiful combination, strong stiff stems high above the foliage   3.00   1.50

Harry Mayer Dec.

One of the very largest dahlias we have had the pleasure to grow. The large blooms were often 10 ins. and more, a very thick flower, and blooms are always large. The color is very attractive, pale rosalane purple, a lilac shade. Splendid habits, very dark green foliage, stiff stems, one of the best   5.00   2.50

Ida Perkins (Perkins) Dec.

Best white to date with me. Profuse bloomer. This clear white decorative won the Garden & Home Builder Medal at Boston for the best New England dahlia ever before shown at Boston. A true decorative with very great substance   5.00   2.50

Jean Hare (Fisher & Masson) H. C.

A beautiful golden yellow, as it matures it becomes an apricot buff, the outer row of petals a golden bronze. One of the most attractive autumn colored dahlias on account of its great size. Awarded a certificate of merit by Dahlia Society of New Jersey   7.50   3.50

Jane Cowl (Down's) Dec.

Deep massive blooms of bronzy buff, and old gold blending darker toward the perfect center. Broad petals with just enough twist to add the refinement so often lacking in the largest dahlia. A stem of unusual strength holds this giant decorative over a bush of ideal growth. Foliage of a thick leathery kind   10.00   5.00

Jersey's Ideal (Waite) Dec.

The color of this variety is best described as lavender pink, although sometimes it is nearer lavender, the flowers are borne face up on top of the stem, the long petals falling down and making a very deep flower, a very vigorous grower and a free bloomer, and an ideal stem   5.00   2.50

Jersey's Beacon (Waite) Dec.   Tuber Plant

A chinese scarlet with paler reverse, one
of the largest and thickest in our garden,
fine stem.   A large basket of these was
the delight of most of the people at the
Big Boston Show   2.00

Jack O'Lantern (Success)

This is one of the Garden and Home
Builder's Honor Roll dahlias. It is a true
decorative with open petals of bright
orange red, shading to a dark spanish red
near the center with gold tips to the petals
that form the center.   The large blooms
are carried on perfect stiff stems looking
one in the eye, very free bloomer   7.50   3.75

Jersey's Beauty (Waite) Dec.

Finest true pink decorative dahlia that
we have ever grown. It is a beauty. All
that has been said of it is true.   Flowers
of perfect form on stiff stems, 3 to 4 feet
long holding the flower high above the
foliage. One everybody looking for a cut
flower should have   .   1.00

Jersey's Mammoth (Waite) H. C.

A monster, color a rich golden mahogany.
A winner at the shows   2.50

Junior (Seal) Dec.

An enormous flower of pure lavender, this
dahlia is one of the best from California,
no collection is complete without it   1.50

King Tut (Seal) Dec.

An extra large blossom of rich dark
velvety, glowing crimson burgundy, of
fine formation, long stems, wonderful
cut flower   2.00

Kemp's Violet Wonder (Kemp) Dec.

The best Violet colored dahlia to date.
The predominating color is violet with an
underlying tone of royal purple. Reverse
is bluish violet.   Flowers are as nearly
perfect in form as possible.   A true
decorative of massive proportions, a very
deep flower on long stiff stems.   A good
keeper both on the bush and when cut   10.00   5.00

Lavendula Dec.

I consider this to be the best large flowered
lavender dahlia I have seen.   The color is
a pleasing shade of lavender throughout.
It is a strong grower with fine stems and
habit, and was universally admired by all
who saw it in bloom. Height, 5 ft.   3.50

La Roda Dec.   Tuber Plant

Silvery rose pink, large well formed
flowers held erect on strong stems   10.00   5.00

Little Jewell Dec.

This miniature decorative was one of the
hits of all shows where we exhibited, and
also in our garden. It is a wonderful cut
flower and in appearance it resembles a
carnation   1.00

La Coronne Dec.

This is another of these wonderful miniature decoratives but is white, and fine
for cut flower, no larger than a Pom Pom   1.00

Lillian Baldwin Dec.

A dark red on fine stems, profuse bloomer,
fine cut flower because of its good keeping
qualities   2.50

Lillian Cambeli (Harding) Dec.

Color a clear pink, and splendid variety
for exhibition or cut flower. A very
attractive variety. In addition to superb
color, it has form and substance to
recommend it   2.50

My Maryland (Down's) H. C.

A beautiful hybrid cactus, delicate pink,
with the faintest suggestion of lavender.
The petals are tipped with ivory and are
pointed, whorled and twisted in a daintily
attractive manner all their own. The
bloom is large, the stem is good, and the
plant is one of those rugged bushes with
leather-like foliage   10.00   5.00

Metropolitan (Mendonsa) Dec.

Bright crimson, evenly tipped white with
veining of gold running to base of petals.
A constant bloomer of large flowers on
good stems. If you were an admirer of
"Pres. Wilson" you will want this dahlia.
This has more substance   7.50   3.50

Marjorie Hennessey (Seal) Dec.

Color amber, heavily suffused with rose,
lightening toward the center to a true
amber. Tips of the unfolded petals are
of a deep rose pink. A fine formation
with long stiff stems   5.00   2.50

Mrs. Shirley Shaw (Broomall-Success) Dec.

Ox blood red shaded maroon, this magnificent flower sometimes has a tendency to
come with a crooked stem, but is admired
by all because of its dark red color and
immense size, one of the largest in the
show kind   10.00   5.00

Mrs. H. E. Loveland (Loveland) Dec.   Tuber Plant

A large pink fading to a more delicate
pink, fine stems, a profuse bloomer, that
actually seems to bloom overnight.   If
you are looking for a cut flower do not
fail to add this to your list, a wonderful
tuber producer   5.00   2.50

Marian Broomall H. C.

Pink and white, descendant of Gladys
Sherwood, it is more cactus in shape than
Gladys Sherwood, with better stems and
habit, a beautiful flower.   Stock very
limited.   Height 5 ft.   2.50

Marean Weller (Marean) Dec.

True of type, extra large flowers carried
on long stout stems, color a most pleasing
shade of soft pink, should be in every fine
collection, very much admired in our
garden   .   1.50

Margaret Woodrow Wilson (Fisher & Masson) Dec.

Exhibition type, large size and great
beauty, color is opalescent pink.   Face of
petals creamy white, reverse phlox pink.
Petals are broad and well placed, terminating in points making a thick flower, dark
green foliage, medium height. Our blooms .
on these plants were wonderful   2.50

Miss M. E. Dingee (Brock) Dec.

An enormous flower of color, hard to
describe.   It is a combination of salmon,
orchid and yellow, on the best of stems   3.50

Mrs. Frances E. Bullard P.

Peony, beautiful light pink, flowers of
immense size and borne on rather short
but strong stems in the greatest profusion,
blooms are extra deep and full for a Peony   .
Dahlia.   Height, 5 ft.   3.50   1.75

Miriam Fisher (Fisher & Masson) H. C.

An exhibition Hybrid Cactus.   An orchid
lavender.   Petals are broad at base,
terminating in sharp points, giving the
flower a staghorn appearance.   Flowers
almost as deep as broad, tight centers.
Medium to tall habit of growth, stem long
and stiff   2.00

Manataug (Symonds) Dec.

A dark red, almost black, on long stems
far above the foliage, very fine cut flower   3.50

Monmouth Beauty (Kemp) Dec.

A seedling of Amun Ra. Flowers are very
large and full, a rich salmon orange, with
a metallic gold sheen, and are borne on
long stiff stems.   This is one of our best 5.00   2.50

Miss Cape Ann H. C.   Tuber Plant

A Snow White Dahlia with large serated
or forked petals, large blooms held high
above the foliage on stiff stems.   This
dahlia won a certificate of Horticulture
from   the   Manchester   Horticultural
Society this past season.   A beautiful
white dahlia that has all good habits,
even to a great bulb producer   5.00

Marmion (Mastick)

Truly, among the very largest in our
garden.   Most flowers are dwarfed when
placed near it.   The color is pure golden
yellow, with bronze suffusion on reverse
of petals and a deeper bronzy tone on the
high center, and outlining each petal.   The
stems are good, and hold the immense
blooms gracefully above the sturdy plant.
Marmion is an excellent variety for the
"Largest Dahlia in Show" competition   3.50   1.75

Nancy Hare (Fisher & Masson) Dec.

Color a true old rose or Jasper pink, a
profuse bloomer on fine stems, and a
flower that all our customers want in-
cluded in their bouquet   2.50

Netawaka (Broomall-Success) H. D.

Orange yellow base shading to a jasper
red, reverse of petals a bright carmine.
Large flowers borne on good stems   10.00   5.00

Nanaquaket (Richards) Dec.

This is a beautiful orchid pink dahlia that
is yet new, it has wonderful stems and
fine keeper, a profuse bloomer   10.00   5.00

Nashawena (Darling) Dec.

Petals are a strawberry color, changing
to salmon as the blossom matures.   The
center is a lemon yellow streaked with
scarlet, long stems hold the blossoms
erect, early bloomer   7.50   3.50

Nancy Sue Lang H. D.

Immense star-like flowers, red tipped
gold, larger and stronger grower than
Mrs. E. L. Lindsey, habit of plant is dwarf
and very robust.   A flower that attracts
immediate attention.   Height, 3 feet.
Stock very limited   5.00   2.50

Pride of Monmouth (Kemp) H. C.

A rich golden buff yellow, maize yellow
reverses, flowers are borne on stiff stems,
a most welcome addition to H. C. section   2.50

Paul Revere (Bissell) Dec. Tuber Plant

A very large bright crimson, heavy full flower, good stems, fine all around dahlia. One of the sensations of the Botanical Gardens in New York 2.50

Polar Snow (Marean) Dec.

The greatest pure white dahlia ever produced, fine type, giant flower on strong straight stems 1.50

Pride of Stratford (Meachen & Sherman) Dec.

Predominating color, cadmium orange shading to light orange yellow at the base of the petals, reverse rose doree. Very large flowers held erect on strong stems 3.50

Primula Rex (Broomall) Dec.

Very light cream or primrose color, the flowers are immense with every good quality, one of the best, new 2.50

Queen of the Garden Beautiful (Broomall) Dec.

A gigantic lemon colored decorative, one of the largest dahlias, a flower that fulfills the dream of dahlia lovers. The stems are unusually strong and it is a wonderful keeper 5.00 2.50

Queen Marie (Harding) Dec.

This dahlia was selected by Queen Marie of Roumania to be named for her, while visiting in this country. The color is shrimp pink with yellow suffusion and a distinct reverse of silver. A wonderful keeper 5.00 2.50

Roycroft H. C.

A spiky dahlia almost star shaped, a cinnamon buff, deepening to a tawny russet in the center. One of the first to bloom, low growing bushes, a profuse bloomer, fine stems 2.50

Robert Scott (Brock) Dec.

Color apricot yellow, rose shading, large bold flower, excellent stem, bushes hold many large blooms at one time 2.00

Siskiyou (Broomall) H. C.

Pink tinged mauve, has created a sensation wherever shown, fine stems, winner of the largest bloom in all the shows 2.00

Sagamore (Kirby) Dec.

A lovely golden color, strong stems, great keeping qualities, wonderful cut flower, a shade in great demand 2.00

Santa Ana Dec.   Tuber Plant

Salmon Rose and gold.   Large flower
with good stems.   Plants only   1.75

Sanhican's Peach (Fisher & Masson) Dec.

A fluffy decorative of good size and great
charm. Color shade of a ripe California
peach with a real peach-cheek glow. Its
oddly twisted petals further enhances its
beauty   5.00   2.50

Sanhican's Nymph (Fisher & Masson) Dec.

Color a beautiful rich primrose yellow,
with the reverse of petals faintly touched
with fawn rose, a perfect stem   -   7.50   3.50

Spottswood Beauty (Broomall-Success) Dec.

A beautiful pink dahlia, color is a clear
Chatenay pink with a slight shading of
lemon yellow at base of petals. Long
cane-like stems   7.50   3.50

Summer (Loveland-Lufkin) Dec.

Color, one of those golden autumn shaded
dahlias, very large and thick, on good
stems. A Derrill Hart Honorable Mention
Dahlia for 1928   5.00   2.50

Silverado (Jessie L. Seal) C.

A long petaled flower, white with lavender
shadings at the center, without the
lavender would not be so impressive, but
with the shadings it is a beautiful flower   5.00   2.50

Shirley Eileen Shattuck Dec.

This prize winning silver cup seedling is
one of the best orchid-lavenders there is.
A large clean clear lavender, nicely con-
structed. Stems long and strong. Free
bloomer   7.50   3.50

Sanhican's King (Fisher & Masson) Dec.

An exhibition decorative of a bright tawny
gold, shading to a bronze center, stems
are slender, black and stiff, tall-growing
plant, excellent keeper when cut, very
tight centers. A fine 1927 introduction   2.50

The Emperor (Marean) Dec.

A maroon of the finest type. The flower
is made up of long flat petals, color does
not spot under any weather conditions   2.00

The Boy Scout (Marshall) H. D.   Tuber Plant

Very large, flesh pink with light cream
at center, best of stem   5.00   2.50

The Lemonade (Ward) Dec.

Here is one of the finest dahlias that has
come out of New England and every good
quality that a dahlia can possess. A large
clear yellow decorative of regular formation, and very good keeper, good stems
and large flowers.   Another that should
be in your collection   3.50   1.50

The Flying Ambassador (Marshall) Dec.

Very large white with a touch of lavender
at back of petals, best of stems, free
bloomer   5.00   2.50

The Pirate (Brock)

A massive well formed flower, a deep
maroon crimson color almost deep purple,
fine stems the same as all of Mr. Brock's
introductions   5.00   2.50

Thief of Bagdad (Loveland) Dec.

Large orchid pink shaded dahlia, very hard
to describe, outer edge of petals are
darker, and blend to a lighter shade
towards center, very pretty and different,
good stems   3.00

The Cardinal (Brock) Dec.

Large bright red decorative dahlia, best of
stems, the flowers are large and deep.   Plants   2.50

The Telegram (Marshall) Dec.

This is one of the first to bloom and was
talked about more than any other dahlia
in the Garden. It is new and has not been
advertised to any extent.   The color is
orange and white, fine bloomer, grows
high, bush is covered all season with
orange and white blooms making a
wonderful sight   2.50

The Clansman (Richard Mills) Dec.

A bright copper orange, a pure color
without any shades or blends, and very
distinctive.   An excellent grower, fine
flower for house, garden, or commercial
use   7.50   3.50

Uncle Remus Dec.

Rhodamine purple (rosy purple), large
flowers on strong stems, an extra strong
grower. Height, 5 ft.   5.00   2.50

Uncle Tom (Success-Adams) Dec.   Tuber Plant

 The nearly black color would attract any
dahlia lover. The flowers are very large
and are held erect on very stiff stems,
looking you straight in the face   2.00

Valentino (Bessie Boston) Dec.

 Color a true salmon pink shading to cream
at the center. Flower has enormous size
and attractive form.   Plants only 5.00

W. J. Erwin (Brock) Dec.

 No doubt this is the best lavender purple
produced. It surely has size, the best of
stems, and is a very free bloomer. One
that all dahlia growers should have 2.00

World's Best White (Murphy) Dec.

 Very large white blooms far above the
foliage, with extra long stems, a profuse
bloomer, a fine cut flower   2.00

Wonderland (Bissell) Dec.

 One of the largest, chocolate maroon with
silver reverse, a new odd twist in each
petal making the flower large and heavy.
Strong growing plant with strong stems 3.00

Waldheim Sunshine (Peacock) Dec.

 A true deep yellow that shows up yellow
under artificial light. The reflex is darker
and there is a rich golden suffusion around
the beautiful, full, high center. Stem is
long and stiff and is a free bloomer 15.00 7.50

Watchung Sunrise (Smith) Dec.

 Color a gold, suffused with pink, a large
flower on good stems, one of the new ones 5.00 2.50

William H. Hogan (Seltsam) Dec.

 Color a garnet red with white tips running
down the center of petals, perfect stems.
Nothing like it so far in dahlias 7.50 5.00

Yellow Princess (Fraser) Dec.

 One of the largest yellow dahlias on the
market. It really is huge, on stiff cane-
like stems   7.50 3.50

SPECIAL Dahlia Collections

Special bargain collections offer the opportunity of obtaining a choice collection of the finest varieties at reduced prices.

We offer these collections from $10.00 to $25.00 a dozen, all guaranteed to be true to name and growth, all varieties to be found in this catalog.

$25.00 Collection

1 Plant each of the following:

Jane Cowl	Jean Hare
Harry Mayer	Fort Monmouth
Ida Perkins	Kemp's Violet Wonder

with six other beautiful varieties.

$15.00 Collection

1 Plant each of the following:

Edna Ferber	Jack O'Lantern
Fort Monmouth	The Clansman
Silverado	Ida Perkins

with six other beautiful varieties.

$25.00 Collection Tubers

1 Tuber each of the following:

Fort Monmouth	Ida Perkins
Nancy Hare	Miss Cape Ann
Robert Scott	Marmion

with six other beautiful varieties.

We also have a $10.00 collection and a $5.00 one in plants or tubers.

Many of the above are listed in our catalog at $2.00, $3.00, and $5.00 each.

A list of well known dahlias that do not need to be described:

Ambassador
Amun Ra
Alex Waldie
Bashful Giant
Ben Wilson
Champagne
Elsie Oliver
Gladys Sherwood
Harlan
Judge Marean
Judge Alton B. Parker
Mrs. I. de Ver Warner
Mrs. Carl Salsbach
Mr. Crawley
Mrs. Ethel F. T. Smith
Paul Micheal
Roman Eagle
Rosa Nell
Siskiyou
St. Bernard
Sanhican Rose
Shudows Lavender
Snowdrift
Wizard of Oz
Walter Hindley
Wm. Slocum

We have a fine collection of Singles, Coltness Gem, and Pom Pom dahlias. If you are interested, write us.

References

The American Dahlia Society
The California Dahlia Society
The Dahlia Society of New England
The Southern California Dahlia Society
The North Shore Horticultural Society
Mass. Horticultural Society
Gloucester Safe Deposit & Trust Co.
Gloucester National Bank
National Association Commercial Dahlia Growers

CPSIA information can be obtained
at www.ICGtesting.com
Printed in the USA
BVHW041159080219
539812BV00018B/1048/P

9 780666 992529